T0023114

MOUNTAIN
AMNESIA

The Colorado Prize for Poetry

Strike Anywhere, by Dean Young
selected by Charles Simic, 1995

Summer Mystagogia, by Bruce Beasley
selected by Charles Wright, 1996

The Thicket Daybreak, by Catherine Webster
selected by Jane Miller, 1997

Palma Cathedral, by Michael White
selected by Mark Strand, 1998

Popular Music, by Stephen Burt
selected by Jorie Graham, 1999

Design, by Sally Keith
selected by Allen Grossman, 2000

A Summer Evening, by Geoffrey Nutter
selected by Jorie Graham, 2001

Chemical Wedding, by Robyn Ewing
selected by Fanny Howe, 2002

Goldbeater's Skin, by G. C. Waldrep
selected by Donald Revell, 2003

Whethering, by Rusty Morrison
selected by Forrest Gander, 2004

Frayed escort, by Karen Garthe
selected by Cal Bedient, 2005

Carrier Wave, by Jaswinder Bolina
selected by Lyn Hejinian, 2006

Brenda Is in the Room and Other Poems,
by Craig Morgan Teicher
selected by Paul Hoover, 2007

One Sun Storm, by Endi Bogue Hartigan
selected by Martha Ronk, 2008

The Lesser Fields, by Rob Schlegel
selected by James Longenbach, 2009

Annulments, by Zach Savich
selected by Donald Revell, 2010

Scared Text, by Eric Baus
selected by Cole Swensen, 2011

Family System, by Jack Christian
selected by Elizabeth Willis, 2012

Intimacy, by Catherine Imbriglio
selected by Stephen Burt, 2013

Supplice, by T. Zachary Cotler
selected by Claudia Keelan, 2014

The Business, by Stephanie Lenox
selected by Laura Kasischke, 2015

Exit Theater, by Mike Lala
selected by Tyrone Williams, 2016

Instead of Dying, by Lauren Haldeman
selected by Susan Howe, 2017

The Owl Was a Baker's Daughter,
by Gillian Cummings
selected by John Yau, 2018

Magnifier, by Brandon Krieg
selected by Kazim Ali, 2019

Night Burial, by Kate Bolton Bonnici
selected by Kiki Petrosino, 2020

Study of the Raft, by Leonora Simonovis
selected by Sherwin Bitsui, 2021

Human Is to Wander, by Adrian Lürssen
selected by Gillian Conoley, 2022

Mountain Amnesia, by Gale Marie Thompson
Selected by Felicia Zamora, 2023

MOUNTAIN AMNESIA

POEMS

Gale Marie Thompson

The Center for Literary Publishing
Colorado State University

For information about permission to reproduce
selections from this book, write to
The Center for Literary Publishing
attn: Permissions
9105 Campus Delivery
Colorado State University
Fort Collins, Colorado 80523-9105.

Printed in the United States of America.

Lines from "Court," by Molly Brodak,
reprinted by permission of the Estate of Molly Brodak.

Library of Congress Cataloging-in-Publication Data

Names: Thompson, Gale Marie, 1986- author.
Title: Mountain amnesia : poems / Gale Marie Thompson.
Description: Fort Collins, Colorado : The Center for Literary Publishing,
    [2023]
Identifiers: LCCN 2023033176 (print) | LCCN 2023033177 (ebook)
    ISBN 9781885635877 (paperback) | ISBN 9781885635884 (ebook)
Subjects: LCGFT: Poetry.
Classification: LCC PS3620.H664 M68 2023 (print) | LCC PS3620.H664
    (ebook) | DDC 811/.6--dc23/eng/20230807
LC record available at https://lccn.loc.gov/2023033176
LC ebook record available at https://lccn.loc.gov/2023033177

The paper used in this book meets the minimum requirements of
ANSI/NISO Z39.48-1992 (Permanence of Paper).

Please don't confront me with my failures
I had not forgotten them
       —Jackson Browne, "These Days"

Animals are closer to god, of course; this is
because animals have no need of god.
       —Lauren Groff, Matrix*

when sun rises
on the trash

the story has evaporated. So no,
to answer your question,
there were no laws.
       —Molly Brodak, "Court"

Contents

III

IV

I

The Divide

It seems important to know the name
for this smallish mountain. What cleave
could take me on, wounded in an
under-the-porch way, still marked
with the blueprint of a predator: feet sleek,
evolved to mimic the prey it longs for.
Like how the feet of foxhounds
resemble those of foxes. In March I ask
a neighbor, *Is there another side to this gap?*
Am I on the wrong mountain? I see no evidence
of when the laurel blooms, just leaf
after leaf in the forever present. I search
for Bosnian recipes on the internet,
watch as the bellflowers plait their way
through the glossy dog shit of my yard.
Mine is a ground problem. Nothing to do
with the mountain I moved to. The dog screams
with the fox as if full of holes blown clean.
I cut off my sleeves. There is no one on the other side.
My friends are sick, and I will never know.

Dummy Prayer

Let me begin   with the weight of sleep
with a cheeky look to my mother   with a wounding

with nine words for pardon   This is what I would wish for
to burrow through   this cycle   like a vole in the yard

and emerge   a new myth   hungry and swirling
after a long night   of no heartbeat   no wakeful pupil

pulsing under my thumb   This is what grief   could be like
its clever enamel   Instead it is   a blue bowl

it is jealous   nothing but a beating   a deep shoulder bruise
from breaking open   my own door   It is eating

and eating   the body   a retreating vehicle
to mark time   the hot milk   rag slack   of comfort

I want the first eight salutations   want Jupiter
as viewed   from its south pole   I am about to recite

the ten plagues   and I need to insert a name
for god   any name   any god

They Make Some Things Easier Here So That Other Things Get Harder

Who will be with you as you become?
I am not asking for me,
but for the girl character who waits
behind my eyelids, the wild foam of her
that spreads only outwards.
Most of the time I feel her endlessly
gone: the sun stuns my empty shoulder.
My scars turn to milk. Gesture.
Counter-gesture.
I wait to swallow my own
form of mercy. When asked, I describe
where I was as a kind of *sanitarium*.
No longer anything healing,
I run in the cold until I am a dark stain
of copper, the outer ring meeting
the offering breast of the inner ring.
I turn frustration into bodily harm,
rub my skin until the blood comes.
I become heat and breath and pink thrust.
The body has its own memory.
I brush against it when I bathe.
I was at a place where mercy began,
but I didn't really know it.

"Cal, have you ever gone through caves?"

after Elizabeth Bishop

All night in this green world, the impulse
       to disappear: I'm dreaming again of islands

shedding islands, glass eyes and clamshells
       between cold walls. I finger an eyelet

in the smaller room, only to turn over
       some heft of shell, some heavier breast,

lonelier ribcage. Some scientist I find myself.
       I name this *future loss,* a thin bark falling

from where this body keeps touching
       other bodies (it *won't quit),* in refulgence,

in the coffee beans spilled on staircases
       where others *won't wake up they won't wake up.*

Refulgence, cousin of *to shine back.* Only
       on the kitchen floor can I still touch you,

a haptic terminal to harken. Only this,
       simple key, is why we continue the myth

of the hair shirt. I have a small kitchen
       heated by this basin of warm water

and verbena. Look again: do we disappear,
       or do we stop touching? Wake up, diver.

Heave your absence on the green of me.
       Please dive down, please wake up.

A Rank, Bleak Devotion

That violence lies in writing is not so far
from the truth. This is the animal I knew before

I started, whose neck I wished to rub my own against.
She brings the word *mercy* into the field.

Her mouth staggers over the counting, the one
and one and one of bodies soaked in oil. In the blue

of gathered facts it feels the same: splattered
mouth, bloody bulb of the sign. I keep practicing

the problem, *To get back at, to get back at,* the letters
written on a field of dark paper, disorder.

I make lists. I peel olives beneath my skin
and push them out of me. I wake up

in the morning and realize that a sex dream
can also be a sexual assault dream. *Mercy, healing—*

these are words I've never used in a poem before.
Can I write into her, she whose own wool

touches mine? A blunter way to say: am I a body
who depends on other bodies? I make lists.

A loved posture can also be a speech act.
This is how it begins. What will seep will seep.

Sleight of Hand

I am with you now. In the panel molding. Instead
of being suffocated. We are comforted. Pulled tight.
Sang the weakened door.

*

Before, and before. All of this. I know.
That she by the pram looked up. At the light
in the hallway. And called for me. This was
before, before.

*

She died and died and still. I love. The ugly ones.
In the pictures.

*

You have no idea how close. She is. Working
herself into other shapes. Holding ice at my ankles.
The telephone ringing. At a constant. She wants me
so badly. To be pumped by the infinite.

Failed Spell for a Spine

for Tim

In the beginning, I wrote this
in hopes. I wrote this before the city burned,
before we lowered our heads
and went quiet. In the way holly leaves
build their ribs from within, I wanted to spin
something hard and golden inside me.

But it's November again. This time last year
the German shepherd was dead, but not yet replaced.
The bog laurel was showing her ribs.
My uncle was alive. Now there are too many hickories.
They grandstand with their stalks spilling out,
thick as oar strokes, dividing and subdividing
like dogwood, like marriage, like cancer.

Is a spine what goes down, or what extends out?
What are we wrung around?

I read once that the spine is our first tree,
its thick foam of bone-bark dividing
into itself. But now can be the thing to snap
and devour us entire. That chance
is maybe the cruelest law there is.
Neural tube. Moth throat.

The danger, of course, was always
to view it as a dwelling. All of this being alive
is a long course of breaking open
and grinding into the dirt.
I am an idiot, a thin spider of a corpse,
making something called *safety*
out of pinfeathers and leeks

or what otherwise undergirds.
All I have now are the simplest prayers,
like *please give me a baby*
and *let my family live*. I don't know
what I demand. What are we wrung around?

Chester Street, Holding Court

Morning is a ready heft
blue ash   tearing the street open

Inside I am a little creature   nagging at god
Writing lines about scruples
My nutritionist says I fantasize too much
          so I watch the largest icicles   hone into form
I chew on rubber succulents
                            take one pill to rise
Next door   the Christian Brotherhood takes turns
                    shoveling my walk   a gesture I hear
only in the bloody tunnels   before dawn

Someone else follows the snow's accrual
                                    It is incurable
Repetition does not hide
the thing it repeats

I didn't mean to come here forever   reduced to an arrow
Didn't mean the violet room
                    But now I must be answerable to
Account for   so many little decays
                                    root canals
I have a body to care for   That is here
It is disappointing
the patience of remaining alive   and daughter enough
The stab of one second to the next
A dead blue hook

Incorrigible landscape
I had so much to give you
I had wanted to sing out from the middle
To carry on   until our heroine dies

But I am the second

                         of two sisters
of the second of two sisters

No Witness

White cold of the morning
and I am no witness.
My shovel is clean.
This is either the beginning of devotion
or signal failure, I cannot tell,
but still the gray earth mouths and pushes.
I cannot see my edges, cannot tell
how far back the pine woods go.
I ask the world for its bandage
of meaning. I cannot tell.

March killed so much this year
just like every year. I hear that death exists,
I hear it and I hear it,
but I keep my mouth away from the wind,
I keep its noises muddied in the woods.
            I am no witness. I no longer
write it down. My shovel is clean.
This freezing fog tastes
of vinegar, moves around
and outside of me, some sad calf
who tracks and tracks.
I crave grief for its meaning. How lucky
to recognize yourself in the damage.
To say, *That was me. I am okay. I am a trooper.*
I am living through this.
            What can I say: I want to be known.

Does it matter if this weak tree
is a hickory? Does it know its own name? Do I?
It dies, it always dies, will always die,
so what blast of fortune does naming give us?

I used to be so full of meaning. It could
have been called suffering by someone else,
but there were no edges outside of it.
If you are alone long enough,
no one is around to notice any *well* or *unwell*.

The work of staying alive is like holding a pose for years.
I stay stock-still while families have families
        and frames of meaning like dark husks,
and then the years. "There is the puddle," Rhoda says,
"and I cannot cross it." I am in a place
where they fatten you up for the slaughter.
I just want to know if I'm going alone.

Mayday

If I were a dancer
If I were doing my best
I would call you
incroyable
a cherishment
a forfeiture of this world
if this were a wavering day
a sudden surprise
of a day
I would be glad of it
This room too close to me
an empty birdhouse
swaying outside
If I were sharp-edged
a swing set
in the middle of this poem
If I were an object
of a lost and more perfect order
I would like tomorrow
to be over with
only to know
that a day can go on

Blueprint (I)

I wanted to call this *morning* only
to justify its unwashed light, so low as to clot.
Blue are the long, white channels

between each slit of blinds, so many lines
at once on the skin. I have been beginning
things for hours: a bowl of popcorn,

goal of steps, the soft rays of blood
that I welcome, then snuff out. Outside
on the corner, tufts of rabbit fur

minnow away against the ice and blue salt,
leaving an imprint my dog can't help
but smell: its past, blueprint

of wildness, dark fingers blooming
outward. A fight was here, a kill—
one good heart, panicked and re-bled

into the ground. *Cera,* a prefix
meaning *honeycomb, wax tablet:* arteries
of a memory I might have had,

diamond-cut again and again. It carries
the weediness of algae: its very stink
is how it insists on being alive.

The Dialect Remembers

How astonishing it is that language can almost mean,
and frightening that it does not quite.
—Jack Gilbert

Frightening, though, that language can mean
exactly what we want it to mean.
Or, what it wants us to mean. Like when I say
I love you or *I want to die*—how terrifying it is
that those words might be true.
What I mean is, a *cartwheel*
is also called a *Catherine Wheel*, the name for
a type of firework—or the medieval joint-rack
named for Saint Catherine. *A wheel set round with teeth*.
So in the same breath, *the most beautiful firecracker*
also means *my long night of torture*. A long tradition
we have of breaking the body, then delighting
in the sparks it makes. I want to tell that story.
The story of what keeps, and what
keeps moving. The story of the moment
right before the word *crisis*—of the green brink,
of our last fig tree turned upwards
in desperation, which is the only kind of hope
there is. And yes, I do mean *brink,* as in *break,*
the pleasure of a spine cracked open to reveal
a future soft as moss. For anything to emerge
from crisis, crisis must show its face.
But *crisis* is only the beginning. The break.
So we turn its wheel, push our hands through
to the wrist, and watch the minutes pump
and pump. Then—the *brink,* the strike of open slit,
sweetening of ferment, all sugar and sun.
And the painful, florid bloom of passing forward.
A wheel set round with teeth.

Mountain Amnesia

Of all the camps to camp
I am made to stop here: log fern,
mountain maple, double-knob—
Bell Mountain's peak mined gaping
and useless. No longer new
to this valley, I am still stupid
and faithful. I blister the tomatoes
and over the phone declare
this is good news when they move
my uncle to a new hospital.
The lowing cattle make hideous sounds
that I confuse with chainsaws
and processing machines.
Elevation is the only direction here.
My cup runneth over, but who can I tell.

*

If writing this poem means that I must
present myself a formed dark cheek of the whole,
how safe all this production of meaning
could be. This hunger filled by quiet
rituals of finding cause and finding cause.
But I am tired of beating just to beat.

Winter bulbs are forgettable
but sticky with secret energy,
cell walls of potential stretched out
just below the forest floor.

*

Thunder boils dark spots down the valley,
in this pulsing yard, kicks up
        in every room.
I started something like this back at the dunes.
I wanted to write about what it was like to lift so easily
From the world.
What it was like to untether   that I could untether

A kind of colony collapse   of one

*

I am never light, really I am never good. One long
phrase of routine against a line of dark.
            I am a side sleeper   a sieve
like a lamb   a soft-brained little dove
guilty of all the greed and ego

        Without the lyrical subject,
this *I* lifts away from my eyes,
the world. I find it impossible, and yet
that is what makes the world
this world.

    It happens, nevertheless.

*

On *Star Trek,* Data dreams of birds
and doesn't know why
So he paints them
Bird bird bird bird bird

He feels "inspired"   He doesn't have anything
to say about them

but Bird bird bird bird bird

*

There are a few ways of knowing I haven't mastered.
There are a few ways of dying I haven't imagined.
In August the creek rose twice.
When I backed my car into the bridge,
I blamed it on the storm.

The rooster next door is alone
and cries a sloughing crow
deep into the afternoon.
The dog who seeded my thigh with her jaws
follows the scent of her own urine
to a grotto underneath my porch.
Tadpoles clot puddles
left by tire tracks and grow,
scooting along on their new feet

until the puddles dry up
and the grass burns. I settle into it,
the letting go.

*

If I am an animal, I should be
a strong one. I should forgo horns
and single flippers for the hardened skin
around my mouth, red burrow of fingers
resembling steeples.

I used to be something else, a child in the churn
sleeping boldly inward, folded,
un-honed. I have tried to be strong and lonely,
to find the muck-throated god
inside the stone. To feign death was easy.

To be out and away from the world
is not a virtue. Even my face has become something
glass-green and lawless.
A kind of loosening of the cheeks.

*

The rain pulls each leaf away
without pomp, rearranges the air.

My cup runneth over, but who can I tell.

Turnover

In the time it took to produce
this sentence, the spinal

shadow of my house has leaned
its wet angle over the yard

so completely, a massacre
so small—yet loved, like

the family lick of the herd—
that it ripples out into the yard

and to the warrens underneath,
near the moldering orange

with its slack rind,
and the gully's mouth

torn open
like a birthday streamer—

because the earth betrays
as it scrapes away

like some black treadmill,
so that from underneath

races a land so struck
with its own disappearance,

that the folded fawn knows
each strangling ramp is right

on the verge of opening,
and that the dip of hoofprint

bears witness to the jaw
cracked slack,

to colony collapse,
how little and yet

how much it matters
to count the dead.

When the Moon Keeps Rising and My Friend Is Still Dead

I remember hitting that squirrel. More specifically,
I remember the after—

    coming back to where it lay like a crater, hands pink
    and cold-settled under its chin, how the dog

    wanted to take it in his mouth and run,
    far away, and keep running—

    or even after that, the next day, when I came back
    to find it gone, and realized that by any bone-rule

    and law, the night animals have surely taken it
    in their filthy jaws and jubilance, and I couldn't stop

    thinking about what must wait nearby, all day,
    until the moon presses in to take care of this waste—

    the hot pillow of blood by his head, brow
    of tire tread—to take their only meal and unpeel it

    from the world. And I know that the dry wood
    of her body must be nothing,

    or almost nothing, by now, and I know that
    what I try to carry of her falls open in the crosswind.

    So I can bless the bush hog and brush clearing
    in their turning and turning, and I can praise

    the most perfect vermin, hold the world's ugly methane
    to my face, but the bowl empties and empties:

teeth, hair, nerve endings, the bottom drops out.
For all the looking after we do, no earth underneath

takes us on. Some stranger the squirrel's jaw is now,
some wet bones we bleach to make way for new days.

We reduce and reduce, and I find myself counting
as I wait for the faucet water to warm, stalled

at the same crackling devotion,
the endless distance of copper and her—

      and because before, I was only thinking
      rock, rock, squirrel, rock.

Pattern of Behavior

It is hard to write on the thumb
you've bitten to death, hard to name
            any story for what it is. *We are reaching out*
to those with similar unsettling experiences, I read.
            To establish a pattern of behavior. For the moment,
let's call it *theater of vindication.* Let's call it
            the bittergreen of dread. Loud as a pushing
throat, a line of questioning I want
            to want to be asked.

The body keeps its bittergreen
and knows nothing, how a symbol
            becomes too soon an elbow, too-strong
hands in memory circling my undressed neck.
            An archive wants nothing to do with me.
Any memory I catch now is a feral flinging:
            (1) He rag-carried me across a parking lot.
(2) He made sure I knew *what all he could do to me.*
            If he wanted. When the bittergreen cracks,

no one is there: this story's water
only destroys. What kind of courage does that reward,
            to find some little truth? It isn't my courage.
I don't own it. But I have held my own body
            in my hands as if it were a smear
of paint, of blood. I have had to smile
            because I am friendly, held shut tight
and hoped I was wrong. Smile because

I am a rite, a pretty thing on my knees,
and now there is a monument
                    to the violet room he holds court in.

The gag is instructive. I wipe dark oil
                    from myself. I dry roses for grief,
dry roses for witches. I prod to find sensation.
                    We know the end is near when the gods
finally arrive. Time to smother your glass rage,
                    time to draw up its board and tank.
I am so sorry to keep standing. I have stopped singing,
                    and that is my crime.

Poem with Jurisprudence

In the stirring light   I arrange myself raw   break some spell
parallel to what   he took   the yellow stain of a body
her body   mine   a chronic institution   *is there a problem?*   No
memory sits here   It is easy   to hate her
I was an empty snakeskin   a stump   I was given the gift
of opening my mouth   but I returned it   nothing I could say
would mark the difference   between language   and silence
I can't call it *denial*   anymore   it defeats me   the evidence

I am a dumb blue   have no memory for   what he did to
her   what I know   he did   *calm down*   my hands smell
of coal   of inventory   I don't want to write   I want only
to make lists   to arraign   in the hottest water   to settle the
reality of the court   In Latin *implicare*   is to be twisted   woven
into a scene   I am implicare to his two long arms   his navy blue
sedan   Where he was relieved to see   that I wasn't scared
of him   and said that *maybe*   *I should be*

The Law of Jocasta

What could she say? You tried to find
her anger here, split her pelvis
for an umbilical thrill. You tried
to remake her, but she
refused, with her black candle eyes,
to look into the dank rot
of your spring. It takes some time to roil,
but when it does, the yard pivots—
foil-green flies scatter
from their happy, dogshit homes.
There must be an aphorism here
about thunder as discipline,
how its roll and hone engraves
from inside. Even Queen Elizabeth
once remade herself a virgin
in this soggy, pink light. Because
this I know: that even evil men die.
It's constitutional. It's the law.
These are our days of pardon, but
do not treat them with any delicacy.
There are tufts of beauty on the earth,
but the earth is ugly and it will not last.

Ojalá

This is one big sentence
This is another
What moves as the light goes down
the sunbox haltingly near
You go into the woods alone
and I forget that there are woods
and that I can do things in them
First you see the family
and then you don't see the family
The snow bunting of March
shoals in hollow places
This house is all I see
It's just science,
like the mammoth's head
the face of a boy
hearing for the first time
And we were not in love
but round vessels in the snow
blue sweaters asleep in the hallway
So here's hoping
that it is willing
that I am willing
and that I am imagining it
Where the universe is spreading
and thirty miles will do
I want to be embroidered
as if then I could adhere to anything

Expeditions to the Polar Seas

This is when I'd like to see gravity happen.
To navigate the infinite. To push myself
blue-stained against glass, like you,
to see you above the trees in the park.
These boxes are for nesting. The city
is a box I'd like to see again and again.
In the past there were blue cafeterias
and the patisserie, there were teenagers.
Now when you eat you are already gone
and the building is gone and I am surprised
at the number of curls in my hair.
When I have a baby I will be so warm
and the warmth will scare me
and I will move through the world like that.
No more summer to carry us.
There are too many choices and only
so many years to make them in.
Nothing will or can happen until I leave
from here, and I think you know that.
There's no reason not to breathe.
There is no one we will touch.

Crow's Nest

No one is around
as the body settles
the body as it loves
cabinetry
and black beds of salt
a township in rural Illinois
the body as it looks
at moths
filling up the pantry
with their heat
Soon my hip slides out
but I can't stop reading
about cruelty
I am afraid
of getting home
and I am sorry
for all the same things
What I have here
isn't a special want
It is what
you might call me
in front of the animals
as animals are
and tend to do
You couldn't leave now
even if you wanted to
You never expect
the ice shelf collapsing
All this is
is a calling out to you
because with you
I might be able
to take this

Dew Value

All this looking is reciprocal, I can say,
alarmed by a darker weekend of movement,
         of celluloid metaphors and how
striped and dancing we greet each other.
         In this flint you could spend your time
loving something more hesitant, more like
         a crocus, more prismatic in its maze hope.
Instead I find myself dreaming of orange trees,
         reach for half an orange. I take
these thoughts into my undone mouth,
         why can't we get what we are good for,
how you can be all this: lonely, enumerating.
         There is not enough time when you
live this far away. I can love you, but this
         dancing is just a hanged wish to join
face to mouth, mouth to hand, hand
         to Cat Stevens record. I'm gathering
speeding tickets here like pine cones.
         Goodbye to that animal stomping,
that gash of solidness from you,
         another anchor of small stars.
The nighttime on my body breathes.
         The blue ridges of my eyelids fill up
the mirror. We are mostly lonely when we change.
         I can get better and write this again.

Hunger Is the Analog

Man's great affliction . . . is that looking and eating are two different operations. Eternal beatitude is a state where to look is to eat.

—Simone Weil

Outside me is a meat. Less woman than a woman,
waste of a symbol that sucks me
and not me. Can you not see it. Again a June
of fruit flies and dried blood, of peeling myself away
like a red arrow. The only architecture here
is a wakeful accruing of the dead. I hold an ear to it.
When Elizabeth Bishop dyes a baby goat bright red it is an act,
a poem act, and I love her for it. But now I don't know
if it is an artful act or a violence, and now I don't want to write.
Passing a family of unborn figs, I love them enough
to slice them open, slip into their patterns.
The tyrant never was just one body.
Is it simple enough to say that the feeling of *ekstasis*
is to stand outside your own position, when *ectasis* is a dilation.
A stretching beyond the solid of yourself. But once I went
so long without water that I was certain my friends hated me.
Once it was pills that gave me moonface, later moonthighs,
a blue pattern of bulge and sleep. If the body is a dwelling
is an archive, then I sing in its ragged globe. Hunger is on both
sides of the windowpane. Inside the belly. No.
No, I don't mean *the*. I mean *my my my*
until I can legislate my own gaping openness. There is *dilation*
and then there is a *stand-off*. The factory in me
can also be a way of caressing. Draws in to draw out,
drawn to and drawn out. At its root, and bile tight.
I could be in that place.

Blueprint (II)

All I wanted was to stand over sickness,
to beat away at its veined throat

that blooms outward in threads, in blue.
I think of milk in its star-blue glass: always

the same instant of change, its enamel comfort
of silence before the telling. I love it as

a holy, mute thing: dark water drum,
shock of liquid skin in its wait. One second

becomes the puddle we cannot cross.
A fine fruit hangs. In its wake my fingers

draw trees, touch whiter lines where I have
learned to practice and re-practice

the body's wound, where only the brightest
shards remain: most tender ribmarkings.

There was a terrible man who cared for me
but he is now dead, and who are you or I to him

but milk. I am so tired of facing faces, done in
by my own unstill picking. If I cared at all

to say a word I would need to lean into
its stutter. So hear me. No hint arrives

in the counting of incisions. I find myself telling
a feral telling. A fine fruit hangs.

Hand Me My Leather

If I am past mercy, it is only to show
that I can invent laws, too.

Drawn inside the deep pink
of public throat, bless of chain-link,

I remove ten drops from the cup
with my fingers. It makes more sense

to be sacerdotal, to give
frantic apologies for death

and tumors, assault and freelessness.
Deserve a white chant we lesson

and lesson, giving out noble shots
to the chest. We want penance

to be a true seam, rosary
a sentence so blooming we carry it

within us like a key. This is no
easy landscape, bruise of walnut oil

dropped from above. We watch
and still beauty also watches.

Most of what I felt when crossing
the frozen lake was nothing, but still

I made myself my own model
of bravery. I don't know revenge.

I look for aphorisms to wake to,
ask the machine of myself to pull at me

in a way that produces a cry. I want to know
the places where darkness was bought,

what plagues took to an iron chair
like seasons: one by one, after one,

then another one. I am still frightened
by peace. Not even a crocus can be beautiful

without forgetting. The trail is still flooded
with the suffering of others. We remove

ten drops from the bitter throat.
We remove ten drops from the bitter throat.

The Responsible

for Molly

In any legal dispute
there are two named parties.
Flat sides on the blade of *versus,*
stripped open like an impossible eyelid.
But what if the victim is neither party,
if she stands outside the blade
and makes no sound,
taking on all of her small boats?
Because I am thinking of a little girl
I didn't know, once a girl,
but now a dead woman I knew,
just a bit, and the sweet things
about her being alive: lemon berry
shortbread and the backs of knees,
raw dates, the thickest of milk and rage.
I am still watching her tiny body
gloss away. She the victim
of someone else's buckshot orbit.
Who is *responsible,* as in: who
answers for this?
Something happens to the sweet things.
Warnings come like parades
of geraniums—indistinguishable
from the last, but beyond beautiful.
Thank you for this warning, we say.
We look down into the violence
with its sticky red head. It dangles
like a vine—no, it *looms*—
at the end of each sentence.
Nothing is arranged. The day is short
but never ends, only folds in, over.
The rooster's queasy crow starts early

and sickles, and sickles. It's not the boot,
but the hands that make the boot.

My fish are living forever

and I do nothing about it. When I dropped a box of dried spaghetti in their tank, they were thrilled for the touch. I watch them be brothers in their own orbits, bearing witness to the other without the vulgarity of contact. I call them *the boys,* and the boys settle in their tank, bodies cozy with wretched water, wretched walls. We don't do well, but we do—the three of us, digging into the outer coppices of damage, but never enough for revelation. Bone bruise after bone bruise, the world praises our resilience, despite what chews away at us. A doctor tells me how lovely my body parts are each time I am afraid I have ruined one. I can't explain the many years I tried to break this resilience—with each slip and tackle I seemed to be *too tough* to care for, built right to stare ruin in the face. I saw ruin and wanted to be it, wanted a ligament torn enough to deserve it, bludgeoned against a simple desire for the upset. For completion. From bruises to shin bone ladder blades to powder and purge, some cloud of metal exists inside me, surely its own reckless vessel. Something final must happen. Even in death it will take a fire to break me down. And even then, I will fall—resilient— like rain.

Something Like a Stevie Nicks Documentary

Singing about hands means that
I need to see yours right in front of me.
It's not too much or too clear. I'm only
an animal making animal sounds,
knocking all these new words together
and holding my head in your lap.
It's not easy to pretend you're dead
for very long. I wake up morning
after morning in the same door-light,
the same mismatch between
the home I evolved to live in and
my own wrecked backpedaling.
Every time I felt like slipping away
you brought me back, and every time
I'm in the woods there's a moment
when I think I'm lost forever.
I can't see the snow but I know
it will come. You might have saved
my life if I hadn't since forgotten
everything about you.
Knowledge is so lonely. Even sober
I shook on the plane, staring down
at the blood vessels over Virginia.
All these things have lost me. I have
a grand stellar motion, I have instincts.
This morning I scratched my face
while washing it. What kind of abandon,
whatever firewalls distance me
from you is enough of a fair warning.
Believe me. You just have to go
in the room to see it.

Compulsion/Procedures

Who am I to be such a great animal.

I come at nothing but this rubbing thinking: a tightly wrapped
blink and unblink. No memory reverb against the brain,
but instead an empty tube. Slight. A web of light
I have already turned over.

I think I am in a room cusp. I think my cusp is God
telling me something. I dig my tongue
into the chapped places. I dig my tongue
into the sweet center cusp. I think God
is telling me about the cusp, what bubbles and tears.

Not one to deny bone, I lay this ceremony down.

I will not touch the windows, my eyes, locks, fingernails.

I will not close my eyes for the pulse in my ears, and I will not
do it again.

. . .

I show my doctor my ragged cuticles. I show him my shoulder.

He sees me every three months. I know he enjoys my sarcasm. He enjoys
my digging, my chapping, my compulsive organism.

For months I was inside. In a book of dead bodies I saw my cat's striped
tail. The tail again. A dead, dead face of maggots.

Rolled, purple. Lock. Unlock/lock to be sure.

Once a woman made me hold my arms above my head for ten minutes, and then asked me for 75 dollars. This was supposed to keep me alive over the winter.

I gave her a speech about thighs that I don't believe and she sent me away to think more about sharkskin.

. . .

I think more about sharkskin. I think about velcro and its barbs.

I think about the factory and disengage. I think about moving gold bars and heavy batteries.

I touch the line on the other side, and yes.

I think the cusp is something I turn my ear into, I turn my voice into, turn my whole caroling body into.

From here, I fight my own material.

Grief Vectors

I want to lay this out as a joke
             want to joke this, and film
      its unremarkable face.
Propped, I spell out this grief
      in rote motions

             that clutch to others, carve
old voices into the ground
      to converse. It works
          as a code we face, brass
     against that same dark lack.
I practice this labor, make signs
      in a tracery language, I am stuck
on the toyness of it.

      She died, and already
          I had arranged these small longings,
    she being my loss she is *mine*—
my own visible barbed wire:
      a ring around my neck.

        What does it mean to rehearse
    and waste this ceremony,
to stain myself with her, when
     already my own body
        reaches toward the dirt.

Elegy with a Hangover and *The X-Files*

This morning is fucked, tasked. Neither
a moving performance nor stream of split
images pushed to ease this vector.
I put my hands behind my head
like she used to do, and wait to be radioed
through the horrible bird static.
Scully's cancer is finally in remission,
so now they're telling me it's time
to pull back the black moss, to start again
inside this bruise. To cup some early red
hope beyond the flailing. I am just
a cold body thriving underneath.
I guess the brain grieves in two halves,
each one built like an almond,
or a skinned knee. Left, and I only wear
hats beginning with the letter *t*
(tam, toboggan). Right, and I can't seem
to draw a goddamn cardinal for the life of me.
I am affixed to no other hub. This arriving
and arriving at the same solution.
Some way past the molecular.
I cut an apple in half and continue cutting
for years. I calculate what it would take
to buy a lifetime supply of Yardley's
English lavender soap. Chris says that outside
the rosemary is crowding out the mint.
I tell him that the kale keeps dying
and then re-growing out of that death,
taller and taller each time, so that
one day it will be as tall as me, assuming
I will still be my tallness.
A film decays like having a favorite film decays.

When I watch *The Longest Day* now I push away
enemy vectors, wrapped up in nonstop gunfire
and John Wayne's tall ankles quietly breaking.
I want to touch that function. I want to feel
like I could be reached. Like even now
there's a maze of flowering azaleas to crawl
beneath. Like if I wanted to I could dress in red,
cut my hair like a boy, name two cats
Cricket and Little Brother and move into
a kind of calm. Outside now birds are calling
each other family and falling asleep.
Maybe one is a cardinal.

Bodega

I am concerned about the bodega. I want to get it down, to be limited by these cold stars, to walk with cigarettes by the bodega. Our families are there, fundamentally unchanged and received with gladness by the bodega. It's nights like this when I get cranky and wish for bad weather. I can't stand it when you tell me bodega. I'm such a baby in the dark blue periphery. I cried on the bus as we passed the bodega, my feet still above the hallway, not at all feeding the best parts of me. There is a plastic bag of cilantro wilting in the bodega and right now, at this very second, everyone else is growing a little bit taller. Everything's settling before I can get to it. Here I am by the bodega recording beyond what I can record at any given time. I see towns like they are not, films like they are not. Here now I am remembering you by the bodega. Here now I bought you a book although you are not here.

Fallout

when it's time to find a new element
when it's time for you to go
keep your arms crossed in front of you
wear your rings about you

in this our next foggy release
a push through the heliopause
wear your whiteness like a new skin
call it cell death
the starling gone
it is more typical to be empty
so chemically bombed and seared
so dismantled by history

when my white web grows out
it will find your spiral arms
achingly intact
would that I could
that we close the reactors
that we become the blanket of cement
in the forest
lap river water with the pigs and forgotten dogs
that we hide there with the nettles
and watch the *Eagle* land again and again
and are friends for the smallest time

I have asked all the right questions
but all I want to do is say *science*
and wait for a response
it is better to see
the silhouette of the surprise
before it happens

Wishes to Will

This is a song
about two people in a car
but they are not us

And I will sing this about the casement
and gable windows

the ceiling of air above
my house:

A little mechanism for the ages

*

This morning everything behind the screen
was much less interesting
than we thought it would be

A triangle of jets loomed across the sky
woke me up something plenty
I waited for their sound to stop
dreaming something about

little girls picking up baby lambs
something about the act of tumbling
from a door frame into the sea

*

A series of bubbles may be blown
between a pair of rings

of pink glass
of white blouses
of heavy doors

*

You look at me
alone in the door
frosted by the sea

like I have said nothing so far

Here are seven dancers
and their positions
of receiving
Look at how they lift up their shifts
to wash their faces

Everything opens up

*

I must know that you're good
because you have said that you are good

and most of the time I speak
an entirely different language to you
It is right but bewildering

I wanted you to kiss me in the wind
or at least to try

This is the only way to say it

*

It starts out like it's going
to be the same thing
but then it isn't

Radially my face is beautiful
only smaller and not as bright

The Milky Way Is a Snowy White

When I speak
I say different things out loud
like *it is night again in the kitchen,*
and *all these golden days*
A schedule is a moving thing
that you can be behind
or ahead of, and my events
are always shuffling
in the micrographia of things and people
Our beginnings were in the ocean
And in the end
the sun is going to swallow us up
But you are coming over
and I want to display this dream
to a room full of people
so that when we get heavier
we can sink to the floor
and never come up

Blueprint (III)

I have such little mercy for my own
strong myrtle, for the walkway clawed open
by snow. To talk about deleting

deletes nothing, the way that *to implicate*
is a wirework, dead twist of tendons
we knot into our hands. I know

that I couldn't stop seeing the capsule
pulled apart upon reentry, its breath
in strands falling afterward,

each one a beating, beating. This is partly
my crime: claw marks in the watching,
how much *like a movie* it was.

News comes and we are fussy
and quickening until the void calls it back.
We wish to be overheard, make sounds

into soggy linen, stuffed with our own
whereas. I suppose this is how we define
destruction: drill into our gums the outlines

of a world gone. To begin writing,
you must think yourself god,
the *lyrical moment* when the poet calls

themselves *poet*. These eyes watch waste,
are the same eyes as the writer
of this poem, tired of beating

just to beat. We will ourselves, we two,
to look away, to what calls for us,
to what will call to us in the end.

IV

The Crying Men

That I will account for the crying men. That I will account for the bobbing faces of crying men who held such beards among them.

That I will account for the tears of men I shouldered, I shouldered the men, I shouldered them in.

That I smile widest in dread.

That if one is silent long enough, the mouth shapes around what it lacks.

That there was a heightened pitch of toothaches that year: my cheek, full of infection, translated to a murky boil on black and white film. That these toothaches directly correlate to the heightened pitch of men crying, that the men had scented beards of fig, or of persimmon, or that the scent of the crying was like a spit.

That once cleared of pus, my cheek became an open cavern, a vacant floor. That I cannot rid myself of the word *teeming*, their crying, my bacteria: florid.

That one April I held the head of a man who cried. That I held his hot moths against my neck so that I became green in my simpleness, so that I watched him with my green, simple eyes. That he leaned over me like an absent fish, that he still leans now, that he is fragrant. His lean was fragrant, or do I mean fetid.

That I have been loved by the crying men, by the violent men. That I sat before their gates. That I kept one awake during his concussion.

That we watched *Cheers*.

That nothing about evil is new. That it is *monotony*. That now I know the crying was a profit, that the profitable crying was in my arms, that onto my arms you can overlay a map, that a map of sickled men may be overlaid onto my arms.

That evil can exist outside of language, and yet we use language to point toward it. See: the dark lacuna bubbling between the terms *genocide* and *acts of genocide*, hung open like a wild onion.

That the man performing my root canal told me *each infection carries its own unique smell*. That he stubbed my open abscess with flaming clove.

That I am obliged to *fact*, that *I cope with facts and facts*, the aluminum carcass I hold in my teeth. That there is *precedent*. *Analogy*. That there is an *example*. See: exhibit A.

That now I write a shopping list. That I take my cans to the store for deposit. That the dealership has a recall for me. That I do the things and throw away the page and they are gone, bleached, an open cistern.

That I too have been cruel. That *implicated* comes from the Latin *implicare*—to be braided, threaded through the lengthy stanzas of someone else's life.

That *implicare* turns into itself, forests into its own inside. That each fingering from the root extinguishes itself, like a small ringlet of smoke. That I keep my fingers inside the vigil of this word.

That once on the sidewalk a man fell into me and hollered something about my ass, his dick. He called me a *fucking cunt bitch*.

That even evil men die. That even evil men, when I type their names into Google, get obituaries about their devotion to our Lord Jesus Christ and the local football team.

That this one man had called from prison.

That this sentence is *of* after *of* after *of*, and beyond that is the edge of a curb.

That there is a scene in *Frasier* in which Frasier attempts to write his show's jingle with a forty-piece orchestra. *If less is more, just think about how much more* more *will be,* he says. That there are poems like this, and I don't know whether I dislike them or if it is jealousy at their ease of naming.

That writing this is not enough. That perhaps the answer isn't to write the thirty-page poem, but to stop the person who does. That it is perhaps my job to put space between world and creating the world.

That he told me *this is what it means to love you.*

That there are still a number of things I have mercy for. That I must work and eat. That I must still listen.

That the sun crashes against the marble stairs of the courthouse. That still the men breathe easy in their crowned brine, their easy language of royal jelly. That they are still here.

Salvage Operation

Power is everything. Even in movies
the lack machine in orbit boils & persists,
gives shoulder to a clean white fire
that generates what it consumes.
The men watch in hope.
At night the radio counts down to blackout,
closing distance between the pitch lacuna
of the unseen moon & the forever
that crosses behind, blistering
& horribly familiar.

It is more than the listening. It is intention,
the evergreen grin of recovery
that rolls over to greet the sun. Pitch & yaw,
ice on the black. A silent waking.
Upturn pressing its thumbs to the dint
of your hips. This is the machine we bless
at the end of its orbit, simply
on some trajectory to follow blind
until all stands again.

Wind Shear

I have too much hair   but not enough to be considered fur
    I live close enough to a church   to see god
and his friends   leave in the white cold of the morning
    their pause woven   and sloping through sun
but the wind is wicked   a chasm   It prickles the bedrock
    the neighborhood bike thief   it toothes itself
under the urgent organs   under the good priests
    I'm not sure I want   evidence of our humanity
I know   the brotherhood next door   they agree
    their yellow porch pew   lousy with wasps
I watch as the wind takes it   by the root
    a hard crack   against their communal van

In the beginning   I moved here like a switchback
    muck of dog shit   in bags stuck to the bottom
of the can   I moved here knotted   had cut
    my own mountain loose   pared it all down
so I could easily lift right out   I'm not sure one grackle
    has anything to say to me   In winter
I am just another   fat mammal   another recording
    of tire and crock   a mashing of bodies
in the hottest water   I soften terribly

    What is it to keep pointing   if it is now my turn
to give mercy   Do I brandish that kind of alchemy
    I have washed away the cut   but what remains still carries
its own face of dread   deep cavities   in the frozen mud
    I didn't know to know   to save the one after me
Guilt never knew reason   and his face   never washes away
    and still I am sorry   It is a hope that grows
away from me   like coarse hair   How pointing
    at intention   is its own kind of fire

Animal Spotting

What kind of stellar motion
I find in you, what plainer voyage
is what I mean when I say I am taking up
some slack in myself. We are only working
models, small forms of the vessel. We live
in confusion, some selves projected on a screen
where we look alike but act so differently,
like I am always waiting for the moment
when lovers change their minds.
Only yesterday I was kissed on the top
of my head, only yesterday I was baking
lavender cookies and dyeing my hair.
Sometimes whales will leave home mid-song
and return months later to finish it,
as if there had been no interruption.
Dirty water fills up my sink like a lung.
The light isn't so good right now,
but on Sunday we used it to walk us up
through the trees. On Sunday we were far away
thinking of the house and its tiny chisel
and pickaxe, its stray walnuts. I cried
for Joe DiMaggio because sometimes
people aren't in the world anymore.
Let's walk to the reservoir today. We can go
to the valley underwater and sing ourselves
right into being. We can find a new tray of marigolds
and think about whales telling each other *hello*
hello hello over a broad range of frequencies.

I See the Moon (to Sheila, age 9)

I see the moon
a tiny embryo, a pinwheel

against the loudest face
of the sun

I see its one white eye
I see its metal collar

The moon is a bowl
of bone, a dead calm above

I stick my finger into it
and pull away

a lake of paste
ceramic confetti dropping

I try to find you
in the bounce of

the bounce of the light
but there is only

the sweet-faced moon
its beautiful vinegar smell

not a shadow to be found
Where did you come from?

How did you arrive?
What is it like to be named

the thing that you are?
You are somewhere

in this scene with me
It's just that the big

blue glass between us
keeps fogging up

from our mouths
and their big loud heat

Do fish know about the moon?
Do you know about me?

I will be back in an hour
I want to try again

Around us the foxes
make baby sounds

White buds slap
against the empty air

I see the moon
and the moon sees me

I Drew a Circle around a Future Tattoo

and thought *I didn't ask for this*   but I did
    and keep asking: what bottomless gnaw
could I have painted myself with   what soldiered lines

    of itch and growth   What more could I peel
from my body   taut and licked dry   like varnish
    to expose its chewed bark   of scars
the oil rings of a hungrier   tenderer child

    It was all I had   a coat filled with salt
red wool of incision   and the threshing machine
    rustling a myth I can't align   it was all blur
and cotton   and southern factory   the gesture
    of lifting the receiver   with words like
cottonmouth   and *remember the institution*
    When down below the church   at the end
of the tongue   a pink crust   racks of every cell
    dividing itself   dresses still in bags   The dark pool
of memory   it stretches across fields

    I had asked for a body   did not wish
its demolition   her oily crush   but I can still see her
    leaning over silver pools   I see her inhale
and climb   over lit palms   Time holds itself
    in white lines   that now   know nothing
I had promised airships   overhead
    I drew a circle   over my armory

Secret Architecture

I'm not sure if maybe I love you,
or if I can't stand to see myself
in someone else's sleeping bag.
At this point I'm sure that,
no, I don't love you, but still
I say *kin* to talk about us.
This morning everything strange
seemed epic, or epic seemed
strange. It makes me feel certain
that we are not here because
we are good. We make a mess
of being asleep and awake.
We cry when we think of trees
and their canker, what the sky
does so awfully between March
and April. I say there's something
saturnine coming up the coast,
and by this I mean they recently
discovered that Saturn's rings
are actually waving. This makes
me turn and think of you, perhaps
you giving me space enough,
perhaps me giving you. I want you
to watch this ballet of starlings.
I want you to tell me more about
highways, about the act of emptying
yourself completely. I want you to take
a picture of yourself in front of
the warmest monument you can find,
and then again in the same place,
later fruited and cemented over.

The Tramp

Do you who knows me know
that I danced in front
of the mirror this morning
that I pretended to tell you
we were moving to the Ozarks
It is all I know how to do
I think I am supposed to think
about someone else
I think I am out of reach
but here you are kept
in my armoire
your fingers on all the stones
while I build myself
this frayed symbol—
log fern, bantam hen
small enough to be vacant
and arching
but we can still love it
I know that right now
I am wearing a slip
and when Charlie Chaplin
pas de deuxs with the globe
I feel I am a total work of art
I attempt to sleep
with one hand under my hip
You want to speak through miles
I can feel it
How much do you want to know
where things come from
Have you ever even seen
an apricot tree

Points of Contact

One after one. After one. Little lights are lost, little signals, little turns taken. Poached eggs and spelt bread on the kitchen counter. How to open one's mouth, then the pressure to open one's mouth, then nothing but soda water. Being ugly is easier to believe. A frame isn't the right word for it. Where I can see myself into myself. I was born ten days late, and the water came out a copper red. Like a breathing. I have seen the family. I have defined the word *firmament* over and over again. I am not saying something. So much as waking to it. What a wake. What a thing to work with.

&

The baby you have is the baby you were meant to have. After so many years, it is what it is. Please understand that. It's too much. That I can't braid my hair. Into your hair. Cohesion happens first in the cells. And then later when the body stops. So I need you to know what I mean. When I say *the house I grew sick in.* To acknowledge the storm rolling in. I reach out in my aliveness now. Wrap you in younger versions of you. I want to meet your body like my body. In a dark kitchen. This is what you wake to. You are you and you. And I want you all in me.

Deep Blue Sea

Last night when we danced
we were a constellation. A budding.
You may not remember, but someone
was closer than you think. Someone saw you
make gestures you've never made
in all your waking life.

Soon you will want to forgo this easiness.
Physical quantities are inherently fuzzy.
Right now I am curling my hair and listening
to *Swan Lake.* When I am talking to you
I say too much. I need you to sit on my hips
while the blood washes in.
I need all of this trying again to last.

Months pass and no one kisses me
in the sun. I lose my footing. I slip out
of superstition. I see what a girl needs and does
and it is what I choose not to need and do.

I can learn almost anything. I can hover,
move on, hover. A body becomes
more massive once you recognize its space.
Try not to turn it into an object. Try not
to recognize it too soon. The house will be
the same, no matter what you do to it.

Ground Rules

It's June and I turn and turn
my wet leg in sleep, in hopes
of making a poultice.
There is so much to learn here,
in this place where fire does
the kind of good violence we need it to.
Already I have taken to calling
this valley floor *peat,* the most useful
of gathered deaths. Each day
my dog and I nod to the soft,
pulpy rot of the world
from behind the sleek blackberries.
Good work, good work, we say—
meaning *step back, step back.*

It's all still up in the air, I suppose—
how I could sink like a bag
of soap and stone, how I could break
and break ties again.
I've been told that the bog here
is tender, with every intention
of a good green underneath.
I suppose I could call it *my little belief,*
open and stupefied as a pinwheel.
But the things we love
are already over, send off the same
sleek gasses of death as anything else.
There is no satisfaction or defense,
just the true song of collapse.
Our fox announces herself like a star
in wobbling red. She makes
her finite mistakes, then releases them

at the end of her shift. *Step back, step back,*
she says. We fire to raze.

Notes

"Blueprint (I)," "Blueprint (II)," and "Blueprint (III)" were written in response to English botanical artist Anna Atkins's cyanotypes.

"They Make Some Things Easier Here So That Other Things Get Harder" is in gratitude to the Vermont Studio Center and to Oliver Baez Bendorf for the title.

"Cal, have you ever gone through caves?" quotes Robert Lowell's "For Elizabeth Bishop 3. Letter with Poems for Letter with Poems," which directly lifts phrases from a letter Bishop had sent him.

"Failed Spell for a Spine" is in memory of my uncle, Tim Coleman.

"No Witness" is in gratitude to Dr. Daniel Helbert.

"When the Moon Keeps Rising and My Friend Is Still Dead" is for Marni Ludwig.

"Ojalá": Although directly translated to "hopefully," *ojalá* derives from the Arabic expression "ma sha allah," which means "should God will it."

"Expeditions to the Polar Seas" is in gratitude to *Joseph Cornell's Theater of the Mind.*

"Hunger Is the Analog" takes its title from a phrase written by Anne Carson, while considering Simone Weil's views on lack and desire.

"The Responsible" is for Molly Brodak.

"Bodega" was included in *Best New Poets 2012,* edited by Matthew Dickman.

"I See the Moon (to Sheila, age 9)" was written in response to a haiku written by a Miami elementary school student via the O, Miami Foundation's education program.

Acknowledgments

I am grateful to the editors of the following publications in which poems from this book first appear, sometimes in earlier forms:

Poetry Society of America: "The Divide"
Tin House Online: "Dummy Prayer"
Cosmonauts Avenue: "They Make Some Things Easier Here So That Other Things Get Harder"
Banango Street: "Cal, have you ever gone through caves?"
Foundry: "A Rank, Bleak Devotion"
The Bakery: "Sleight of Hand"
Wildness: "Chester Street, Holding Court," "Salvage Operation"
Colorado Review: "Ground Rules," "Mayday," "Turnover," "When the Moon Keeps Rising and My Friend Is Still Dead," "I Drew a Circle around a Future Tattoo"
Conduit: "Blueprint (I)," "Blueprint (II)"
Bennington Review: "The Dialect Remembers," "My Fish Are Living Forever"
The Adroit Journal: "Pattern of Behavior," "Hand Me My Leather"
Birdcoat: "The Law of Jocasta," "The Responsible"
Birdfeast: "Ojalá"
Guernica: "Expeditions to the Polar Seas"
Diode: "Crow's Nest"
Phantom Limb: "Dew Value"
Nightjar: "Hunger Is the Analog"
Sink Review: "Something Like a Stevie Nicks Documentary," "Points of Contact"
Smoking Glue Gun: "Compulsion/Procedures"
Crazyhorse: "Grief Vectors"
Everyday Genius: "Elegy with a Hangover and The X-Files"
B O D Y: "Fallout" (formerly "Emanations")
iO: Poetry: "Wishes to Will"
Ampersand Review: "The Milky Way Is a Snowy White"
Witness: "Blueprint (III)"
South Carolina Review: "Wind Shear"
Columbia Review: "Animal Spotting"

Jai-Alai Magazine: "I See the Moon (to Sheila, age 9)"
The New Megaphone: "Secret Architecture"
Whiskey Island: "The Tramp" (formerly "Sleep")
ILK: "Deep Blue Sea"
Sixth Finch: "No Witness"

Some of these poems appeared in the chapbook *Expeditions to the Polar Seas* (Sixth Finch Books, 2013).

* * *

Endless thank you to my comrades, my first readers, *mis medias naranjas*, Caroline Cabrera and Anne Cecelia Holmes.

This book has been almost ten years in the making, so thank you to years and years of students, teachers, and colleagues—in Amherst, Athens, Grand Rapids, and now Young Harris. Endless gratitude to friends and colleagues who over the years acted as generous readers, correspondents, sources of inspiration, and without whom this book would not exist.

Thank you to the organizations and institutions who provided the time and support to write this book: The Willson Center at the University of Georgia, Kimmel Harding Nelson Center for the Arts, Vermont Studio Center, Grand Valley State University, and Young Harris College.

I am enormously grateful to everyone at the Center for Literary Publishing who helped put this book together. Huge thanks especially to Stephanie G'Schwind, whose kindness made this process both painless and meaningful. Thank you to Felicia Zamora and Diane Seuss for your words and support. I am forever honored.

Thank you to my family.

This book is set in Sabon and Futura
by The Center for Literary Publishing
at Colorado State University.

Copyediting by Tasha Seebeck.
Proofreading by Lauren Furman.
Book design and typesetting by Chase Cate.
Cover illustration by Liz Orton.
Cover design by Stephanie G'Schwind.
Printing by Books International.